AGLAONIKE'S TIGER
© Claudia Barnett
Trade Edition, 2024
ISBN 978-1-63092-143-9

Also Available From
Original Works Publishing

AGELESS by Bridgette Dutta Portman

Synopsis: Ninety is the new thirty at the turn of the 22nd century. When Marin refuses to take the anti-aging drug celebrated by the rest of society, she invokes her mother's ire and risks becoming marginalized in a culture that worships youth, denies death, and treats old age as a malady. As Marin's choice begins to affect not only her but the people she loves, will she find the strength to hold out, or succumb to social pressure?

Cast Size: 4 Females, 2 Males, 4 Various

AGLAONIKE'S TIGER

By Claudia Barnett

Orpheus: I told you not to mention her name again. She almost ruined you, didn't she? A woman who drinks, who walks the streets with a tiger on a leash, who puts ideas in our wives' heads and scares young girls out of marriage.

Eurydice: But that's her religion. It's moon worship!

—Jean Cocteau

Characters
AGLAONIKE—She ages throughout the play.

TIGER—A tiger. Male. Played by a dancer.

ERICHTHO—Female. She wears a wreath of vipers around her neck.

CHORUS 1, 2, 3—Three women. Their costumes are white dresses, the kind of thing a Greek statue might wear. They play all the other roles, regardless of gender.

Casting Suggestions for the Chorus

CHORUS 1	Hekate, Astronomer 1, Oracle, Witch 1, Spectator 1, Warrior 1, Passerby 1
CHORUS 2	Selene, Astronomer 2, Witch 2, Spectator 2, Harry, Warrior 2, Tigress, Passerby 2, Hesper
CHORUS 3	Artemis, Astronomer 3, Yiayia, Witch 3, Spectator 3, Hegetor, Passerby 3, Strix

Setting
Thessaly, Greece, circa 200 BCE.

Music
The play includes three different musical themes:

MOON MUSIC Classical.

TIGER MUSIC Tango.

WITCHY MUSIC Calliope.

Intermission
An intermission is possible (if absolutely necessary) following scene 11.

Aglaonike's Tiger had its world premiere production at Venus Theatre (Deborah Randall, artistic director) in Laurel, Maryland, on September 7, 2017. Deborah Randall directed. Kristin Thompson designed the lights, Neil McFadden designed the sound, Amy Belschner Rhodes designed the set, Deborah Randall designed the costumes and props. Puppet bones were created by Matthew Pauli and masks by Tara Cariaso. Choreography was by Alison Talvacchio. Laura Schraven designed and Olivia Lightener illustrated the graphics. Lynn Bruce served as stage manager, and Heather Helinsky as dramaturg. The company was as follows:

AGLAONIKE—Ann Fraistat
TIGER—Matthew Marcus
ERICHTHO—Deborah Randall
CHORUS 1—Katie Hileman
CHORUS 2—Katie Jeffries Zelonka
CHORUS 3—Amy Belschner Rhodes

Historical Note

Very little is known about Aglaonike, also known as Aganice of Thessaly. She is mentioned briefly in the writings of Plutarch and Apollonius of Rhodes. Historians place her at various dates, from the first to fifth century BCE; some say she was a mythological figure. If she lived, it must have been earlier than the second century BCE, when the availability of the Antikythera mechanism—a device used to predict eclipses—became widespread. Since no one knows how Aglaonike predicted eclipses, I've attributed theories of some later scientists (such as Hipparchos) to her.

Acknowledgments

I'm grateful to directors Blair Cadden, Shelby Brewster, Deborah Randall, and Carol Herin Jordan for embracing this play's challenges and to dramaturg Heather Helinsky for her insights. Thanks to March Forth Productions, the Magic City Reading Series and the Alabama Jazz Hall of Fame, 5th Wall Productions, the University of Pittsburgh, and Western Kentucky University for staged readings, workshop and student productions, and the opportunity to work with the *many* wonderful actors, designers, dramaturgs, dancers, choreographers, composers, and musicians who have contributed to the development of this script, including Eric Webb, Bree Windham, Jason Olson, and Michael McDevitt. Thanks too for the support of Middle Tennessee State University, specifically the College of Liberal Arts, the English Department, the Faculty Development Committee, the Faculty Research and Creative Activity Committee, and the Women's and Gender Studies Program.

One Last Thing

Aglaonike's Tiger is not a children's play.

for Naomi London

AGLAONIKE'S TIGER

Prelude

A bright moon hangs suspended above a dark stage, illuminating it. TIGER enters, prowling, and crosses the stage. When he is about to exit, HE looks back at the moon. It turns red, as if filling with blood. HE exits. The moon turns black. Darkness.

End of Prelude

Scene 1

At rise. Darkness. Suddenly the moon shines. Directly below it, at the point where three roads meet, CHORUS 1, 2, and 3 stand frozen, their backs to each other, forming a human pillar (Hekate Triformis). They wear masks of the goddesses Hekate, Artemis, and Selene. Each looks straight ahead. Off-stage, TIGER roars.

CHORUS 1 takes several steps forward.

CHORUS 1

One road leads to the forest.

CHORUS 2 takes several steps forward.

CHORUS 2

Another to the sea.

CHORUS 3 takes several steps forward.

CHORUS 3

The third to Thessaly.

CHORUS 1

Could one walk, or must one fly like an ibis
to visit the gods on Mount Olympus?

CHORUS 2

(Unfurling a map of ancient Greece.)
The map depicts the land and seas
of Jason, Achilles, and Hercules,

CHORUS 3

but charts neither underworld nor heavens,
realms of magic and superstitions,

CHORUS 1

from whence the goddess of the moon
surveys the world with her triple frown.

CHORUS 2

Like that three-headed hellhound, ferocious Cerberus,
the triformis goddess has multiple faces.

CHORUS 3

She guards the crossroads where three paths converge,
a mythical place where spells are conjured.

CHORUS 1

The Witches of Thessaly claim the deity sanctions
their mystical moonlit machinations.

CHORUS 2

Yet the moon goddess hallows one little mortal:
neither siren nor sorceress but a studious girl.

AGLAONIKE enters holding a wineskin as the CHORUS transforms into three Astronomers. The ASTRONOMERS huddle together.

AGLAONIKE

Greetings, Astronomers.

ASTRONOMER 1

It's a girl.

ASTRONOMER 2

What's she doing here?

ASTRONOMER 3

Has she brought olives?

ASTRONOMER 1

And anchovies?

ASTRONOMER 2

And onions?

AGLAONIKE

Forgive me, Astronomers. I've brought only wine.

SHE hands them a wineskin. THEY are overjoyed.

ASTRONOMER 3

Is that all?

AGLAONIKE

I've come with a question. It's about the moon. You've predicted a lunar eclipse in 29 days, but according to my own calculations, it'll happen tonight.

ASTRONOMER 1

Your ... *calculations*?

ASTRONOMER 2

You mean you do math?

AGLAONIKE

Yes. While the frequency of the lunar eclipse is typically six lunations of 29.5 days, this time it will be five. My hypothesis takes into account the elliptical shape of the lunar path. The moon's orbit is an imperfect circle.

ASTRONOMER 3

Imperfect? Impossible!

AGLAONIKE
My father brought home a Mesopotamian moon chart from his pillaging, and in studying it, I've noted that the five-cycle pattern emerges with some regularity.

ASTRONOMER 1
Have you seen *our* chart?

AGLAONIKE
Yes. That's why I've come to ask you—

ASTRONOMER 2
Who sent you to harass us?

ASTRONOMER 3
Do you have any idea what you're saying?

ASTRONOMER 1
Or what an eclipse portends?

ASTRONOMER 2
Drought!

ASTRONOMER 3
Starvation!

ASTRONOMER 1
Disease!

AGLAONIKE
I was hoping you'd explain the science.

ASTRONOMER 2
The science!

ASTRONOMER 3
To a girl?

AGLAONIKE
I was hoping you'd teach me.

ASTRONOMER 1

Next time, bring pomegranates.

ASTRONOMER 2

Next time, stay home!

ASTRONOMER 3

We don't teach girls.

AGLAONIKE exits. The ASTRONOMERS stare at the sky. The moon turns red. The ASTRONOMERS exit. Darkness.

CHORUS 1, 2, and 3

(off-stage)
It's the end of the world!
Drought!
Starvation!
Disease!
The deaths of kings!
Run for your lives!

Lights up on a kiosk with a sign that says "Oracle." The ORACLE sits at the kiosk. ARTEMIS hands the Oracle a kitten and then poses as a statue. AGLAONIKE enters and kneels before her.

AGLAONIKE

They're saying I caused it.

ORACLE

Maybe you caused it.

AGLAONIKE

I couldn't have caused it. I predicted it.

ORACLE

Maybe that's the same thing.

AGLAONIKE
But that doesn't make sense.

The ORACLE hands Aglaonike the kitten.

ORACLE
Here. This'll keep your mind off your troubles.

AGLAONIKE
Uh, thanks, but I'm not really a cat person.

ORACLE
It's from Artemis.

HE gestures to the statue.

AGLAONIKE
Artemis the virgin moon goddess? She's my favorite.

ORACLE
Then surely you recognize her.

AGLAONIKE
All those statues look alike.

ORACLE
She's been watching you.

AGLAONIKE
Sure she has. And she's giving me a kitten.

ORACLE
If you don't believe in miracles, why consult an oracle?

AGLAONIKE
No one else would listen.

As AGLAONIKE exits with the kitten, ARTEMIS gestures toward her as if casting a spell. Tiger music plays.

End of Scene 1

Scene 2

At rise. YIAYIA at home, sweeping. She's ancient. AGLAONIKE enters with her kitten.

AGLAONIKE

Look, Yiayia.

YIAYIA

You've brought home a cat?

AGLAONIKE

Daddy said I could.

YIAYIA

No he did not. Your father's been off to war all year.

AGLAONIKE

It's just a kitten.

YIAYIA

It'll grow.

AGLAONIKE

I'd like that. Please, Yiayia. I'd like to have a great big cat.

YIAYIA

You would? Why? Are you afraid?

AGLAONIKE

I'm the child of brave Hegetor. I can't be afraid. Bravery is hereditary, isn't it, Yiayia?

YIAYIA

It may be. But being brave doesn't mean you have no fear.

AGLAONIKE

It doesn't?

YIAYIA
No. It means you master your fear. The more afraid you are, the braver you need to be. If you haven't any fear, you have a limited imagination.

AGLAONIKE
Imagination? What about facts? Logic? Data? You've always taught me to trust the evidence.

YIAYIA
The world is a dangerous place. You'll prove it yourself. Just remember: Cat or no cat, when you feel scared, and even when you don't, keep trying.

AGLAONIKE
Keep trying what? You always say that.

YIAYIA
I'm afraid for you, Aglaonike.

AGLAONIKE
Then let me keep Tiger. He'll keep me safe. I'm certain.

YIAYIA
Most girls seek husbands to protect them.

AGLAONIKE
I'd rather have a cat.

YIAYIA
He's just a kitten.

AGLAONIKE
But he'll grow, Yiayia.

End of Scene 2

Scene 3

Darkness. Time passes as the moon twirls through phases. Then, at rise: a treetop. AGLAONIKE and TIGER lie on their backs and stare up at the night sky.

AGLAONIKE

Listen, kitten. Did Artemis pluck you from the heavens? You seem happiest high up. Perhaps we'll go, some day.

Time passes as the moon twirls through phases.

Listen, kitten. See those stars? They're named for the Pleiades. Orion stalked seven sisters, and they escaped to the sky. I see only six. Did he catch one?

Those sisters were seduced by the gods. *Seduced* means tricked. That won't happen to me. I'm an only child, so I've learned to take care of myself. Seven's a lot of sisters. When you think someone's got your back, you get sloppy.

Time passes as the moon twirls through phases.

Over there's Orion with his sword, his club, and his lion skin. He hunted women *and* cats. He'll be hunting us forever.

YIAYIA

(Off-stage.)
Aglaonike! Time for bed!

AGLAONIKE

(To Tiger.)
Come on, kitten. Let's go for a walk.

TIGER looks in the direction of Yiayia's voice.

Don't worry. You'll protect me.

AGLAONIKE climbs down from the tree. TIGER leaps down and stands and roars. SHE considers him.

You're not a kitten anymore.

SHE ties a long red ribbon to Tiger and holds it like a leash. THEY exit.

YIAYIA

(Off-stage.)
Aglaonike? Are you asleep?

The sound of hissing snakes as the stage transforms into a creepy forest. AGLAONIKE and TIGER enter.

AGLAONIKE

Tigers are not afraid of snakes. Tigers are not afraid of snakes. Tigers are not afraid of snakes. Tigers are not af—

The hissing stops. ERICHTHO appears in a cloud of smoke, a wreath of vipers around her neck. SHE stands imperiously in their path. TIGER growls and steps in front of Aglaonike.

Are you a snake?

ERICHTHO

I am the sorceress Erichtho.

AGLAONIKE

The sorceress Erichtho. Vipers are venomous, yet you wear them 'round your neck?

ERICHTHO

Tigers are carnivorous, yet you keep one at your beck.

AGLAONIKE

How did you make the smoke?

ERICHTHO

You ask too many questions. You must be Aglaonike. I've been waiting for you. And your little cat, too.

ERICHTHO takes a step towards Tiger. HE takes a step back.

AGLAONIKE

He doesn't like strangers.

ERICHTHO

He's a tiger, not a puppy. He's so accustomed to your coddling, he thinks he's a pet.
(To Tiger.)
You have no idea who you are, tigrine beast.

AGLAONIKE

We're not impressed with your riddles and snakes. You're trying to scare us, but we're not trembling.

ERICHTHO

You have gumption, I'll grant you. Do you get it from Yiayia's grape leaves?

AGLAONIKE

How do you know my grandmother?

ERICHTHO

It's a pity her powers are merely culinary. She had potential. As do you, Aglaonike, which is why I've lingered in this copse. I come with a proposition.

AGLAONIKE

No thank you.

ERICHTHO

Shouldn't you hear it before you refuse? You're far too impetuous. You'll learn to curb your emotions as you encounter adversity. To that end, I propose to take you on as an apprentice. If you can tame a tiger, you can cast a spell.

AGLAONIKE
Apprentice in sorcery? I don't think so. I want to learn science.

ERICHTHO
I've made you a better offer. Consider with care. A period of indenture could lead to infinite erudition. Is that not your prime objective?

AGLAONIKE
You're trying to trick me into telling how I caused that eclipse.

ERICHTHO
You haven't been listening. I offered to teach you. And I know you didn't cause that eclipse: That's not in your power. Though some say the eclipse occurs when an animal eats the moon.

AGLAONIKE
You mean Tiger? You think Tiger can cause an eclipse? You think he's supernatural.

ERICHTHO
How do you explain a tiger in Greece?

AGLAONIKE
Alexander the Great had one.

ERICHTHO
You compare yourself to a king?

AGLAONIKE
My tiger could be his tiger's grandson.

ERICHTHO
His tiger was male. And solitary. He spawned no descendants. Alexander brought him home from Asia, a tribute from his vanquished foes. That tiger gazed at the sky with longing: lonesome, impotent, fattened with bloody meat.

AGLAONIKE
You sound as if you remember, yet you can't be *that* old.

ERICHTHO
Your youth is a simple fact; my age is an achievement.
My life has spanned centuries. Don't twist it to insult me.

ERICHTHO grabs a viper and tosses it at Aglaonike. TIGER races to intercept. The viper vanishes mid-air.

AGLAONIKE
What happened? Where'd it go?

ERICHTHO
Magic.

AGLAONIKE
I don't believe in magic.

ERICHTHO
You saw it with your own eyes. Isn't that what you call "empirical evidence"?

AGLAONIKE
I call it a trick.

ERICHTHO
What of the gods? Do you doubt them, too?

AGLAONIKE
The gods watch over me.

ERICHTHO
You believe what's in your best interest.

AGLAONIKE
I know you're no god.

ERICHTHO
When you come to your senses, remember my name.

With a dramatic flourish, ERICHTHO disappears in a cloud of smoke.

AGLAONIKE

Erichtho: vaporized. Impressive. I'd like to learn to do that.

AGLAONIKE sniffs the air.

Smells like rancid quail eggs.

AGLAONIKE waves her arm through the air.

Feels like frosty winter.

TIGER sniffs the ground and tries to track ERICHTHO's scent. HE crawls in circles and stops. AGLAONIKE kneels beside him and examines the ground where Erichtho stood. SHE rubs her hands against the ground and tastes her fingertip.

Tastes like honey mead. A recipe for smoke? I'll unravel the formula, uncover the catalyst, pinpoint the proportions. Maybe I can do *that*.

SHE stands and poses as Erichtho.

How'd I look with vipers 'round my neck?

TIGER growls.

You're right. Who needs snakes when you've got your own tiger?

SHE kisses Tiger, picks up his leash, and leads him away. The hissing resumes.

End of Scene 3

Scene 4

Darkness. Time passes as the moon twirls through phases. Then, at rise: A tent with a door in front and a hole on top. A rope-and-pulley system is hooked up at one side. In front of the tent, a sign: "Lunar Eclipse. 5 Drachmas." WITCH 1 and WITCH 2 sell tickets. They are puppets. WITCH 2 wears an eye patch. AGLAONIKE and TIGER approach.

WITCH 1
One night only!

WITCH 2
Standing-room only!

AGLAONIKE
A lunar eclipse? Tonight? That's impossible.

WITCH 1
Not impossible at all.

WITCH 2
Our sorcery is strong.

WITCH 1
We're the Witches of Thessaly. Haven't you heard of us?

AGLAONIKE
Witches? Then you must know Erichtho. I've been wanting to ask her—

WITCH 2
We draw the moon down to the ground.

WITCH 1
Where it emits its lunar froth.

WITCH 2
That noxious ooze that coats the ground at daybreak.

AGLAONIKE

That's ridiculous.

WITCH 1

Not ridiculous at all.

WITCH 2

Terrifying, maybe.

WITCH 1

Unless you're a believer.

AGLAONIKE

A believer in what?

WITCH 1

That'll be five drachmas.

AGLAONIKE hands Witch 1 some money and begins to enter the tent, pulling TIGER by his leash.

WITCH 2

No pets allowed.

TIGER sits beside the door. AGLAONIKE nods at him and enters the tent. WITCH 1 and WITCH 2 follow her. Witchy music plays.

Lights up inside the tent: a puppet theater. WITCH 1 and WITCH 2 are on stage. Their audience is a mass of bobblehead silhouettes.

WITCH 1

Ladies and gentlemen, welcome to tonight's enchantment of the moon. And now, at mortal risk to ourselves and our standing with the gods—

WITCH 2

Last time, I lost an eye!

SHE holds up her eye.

WITCH 1

(As if reciting a dramatic monologue.)

—my sisters in sorcery will charm the moon into darkness and lower it to the Earth.

The sound of cymbals clashing (off-stage). As WITCH 1 and WITCH 2 speak, outside the tent WITCH 3 (human) enters with a spray bottle and a set of cymbals, which she places on the ground. SHE starts fiddling with the rope-and-pulley system, causing a cover to spread slowly, squeakily, across the hole in the roof.

WITCH 1 *(continued)*

The moon crosses the sky in various guises: disk, crescent, hemicycle. With unearthly magic, she mitigates darkness so we may navigate night. Like a celestial magnet, she draws the tide towards our beaches as she crosses the sky. In the absence of sunlight, the moon reigns supreme.

WITCH 2

Three goddesses converge in the moon. Selene in the sky. Artemis on Earth. And when the world is wrapped in blackness, like a Cimmerian cave, Hekate overshadows all. Darkness is her domain.

When the hole is completely covered, witchy music stops playing. Sounds of ooh and aah from the audience.

WITCH 1

The moon has descended to Earth. Ladies and gentlemen, we now enter the blackest moments of our journey—our blind tour of the underworld as we motionlessly descend. Eyes open or closed, you see blackness. Listen to the ripples of the River Lethe. Feel the dewy souls of the dead. Fathom. In. Silence.

Outside the tent, WITCH 3 picks up the cymbals and clashes them together. The bobbleheads bob. Silence. WITCH 3 retrieves her spray bottle and sprays the ground. TIGER watches her. SHE considers spraying Tiger. HE stands as if to growl. SHE places a finger over her lips. Witchy music plays.

Ladies and gentlemen, beseech the dark goddess. The moon will rise again. What will you sacrifice for coruscation? Will you promise your love? Will you pledge your soul? Will you contribute cold, hard cash?

As WITCH 1 speaks, WITCH 2 floats about with a collection plate, and coins are tossed in it. Outside the tent, WITCH 3 fiddles with the ropes and pulleys, and re-opens the hole. More oohs and aahs from the audience. WITCH 3 exits with her cymbals and spray bottle. Witchy music stops.

WITCH 2

Thank you for coming, and have a nice day.

THREE spectators emerge from the tent.

SPECTATOR 1

That was terrifying.

SPECTATOR 2

Exhilarating.

SPECTATOR 3

Worth every drachma.

SPECTATOR 1

I've never felt so clean.

AGLAONIKE emerges from the tent.

AGLAONIKE

(To Tiger.)
There wasn't any science. There wasn't even witchcraft. They just covered the hole in the roof so we couldn't see the sky.

SPECTATOR 1

(Pointing to a spot on the ground.)
Noxious ooze! The moon left venom in its wake! Ahhhhhhhhhhh!

SPECTATOR 1 runs off screaming. AGLAONIKE kneels and touches the spot on the ground.

AGLAONIKE

Venom? Sticky.

SHE holds up a finger to the Spectators and tastes it.

Carob molasses? I could do better than that.

SPECTATOR 2

The girl has no modesty.

SPECTATOR 3

No reverence.

SPECTATOR 2

No fear.

SPECTATOR 3

Don't you remember? We knew her in school.

SPECTATOR 2

Girls don't go to school.

SPECTATOR 3

She snuck in. Dressed as a boy.

AGLAONIKE

And I scored higher on exams than you. Tiger?

TIGER approaches Aglaonike and nuzzles her.

You were out here when the moon "descended." How'd you avoid the venom? Shouldn't you be coated with ooze?

(To the Spectators, as she pets Tiger.)

Not sticky. No lunar suppuration on Tiger.

SPECTATOR 2

You ought to be ashamed.

TIGER growls at the SPECTATORS, who run off in fear.

AGLAONIKE

(To Tiger.)

I'm glad the moon didn't get you.

WITCH 1 and WITCH 2 emerge from the tent. Witch 2's eye patch dangles around her neck, and there's a hole where one of her eyes should be.

WITCH 1

(To Witch 2.)

Sister, your oculus.

WITCH 2

(Popping her eye back in place.)

Oops. I forgot. Again!

(To Aglaonike.)

Show's over.

AGLAONIKE

You didn't draw the moon down. You didn't even try.

WITCH 1

Why would we try?

WITCH 2
Are you questioning our witchcraft?

AGLAONIKE
I'm questioning your science.

WITCH 1
Science? We're witches.

AGLAONIKE
I could do better than that.

WITCH 2
Is that a challenge, little girl?

AGLAONIKE
It's a fact.

WITCH 1 and WITCH 2 cackle.

End of Scene 4

Scene 5

At rise. Noon. TIGER lies in the treetop and stares up at the sky. AGLAONIKE stands below and holds up her hands as if to frame the sky. SHE tries her hands in different positions, creating shadows on the ground.

AGLAONIKE
It's all about shadows. They change. Time of year, time of day: You won't see stars at noon.

TIGER stares at the sky.

Listen, kitten. I need you. I know you're nocturnal, but it's important.

TIGER takes one last look at the sky and hops down.

You know the drill.

TIGER checks the ground and positions himself.

Stand straight.

TIGER stands straight. AGLAONIKE uses a red ribbon to measure Tiger's shadow. SHE makes a mark on the ground where it ends.

Relax.

SHE holds up the ribbon and indicates an inch at the end.

Shorter. This much. Every day exactly this much. You're not still growing, are you? That would interfere with my calculations.

SHE folds the ribbon in half and considers it.

We're almost at equinox, when the scales of Libra balance. I predict that in two days, the lengths will be equal. After that, the shadows will get longer. That means … springtime!

TIGER roars with delight. Tiger music plays. HE stands and holds out his arms to Aglaonike. THEY tango. They're good.

Enter ARTEMIS (played by ERICHTHO instead of Chorus 3). SHE is the source of the Tiger music, which she plays with a lyre. SHE continues to play as SHE observes the dance. When SHE stops playing, TIGER and AGLAONIKE stop dancing. AGLAONIKE gasps and kneels to the goddess. TIGER kneels, too.

Mighty Artemis. I recognize you from your statue. But weren't you taller?

A clap of thunder.

I admit I was skeptical, goddess, but I see you standing before me, and I heard your music play. My kitten's grown into my Tiger. How can I express my thanks?

ARTEMIS spins and transforms into ERICHTHO.

The sorceress Erichtho?

ERICHTHO

The necropolis at midnight. Bring the cat.

ERICHTHO exits.

AGLAONIKE

Impersonating a statue. That's cheap. But did you notice, Tiger? She cast no shadow.

The sound of hissing snakes.

<u>End of Scene 5</u>

<u>Scene 6</u>

At rise. The necropolis. HEKATE, SELENE, and ARTEMIS pose as statues and hold candles (unlit). Silence. A full moon lights the sky. AGLAONIKE and TIGER enter. AGLAONIKE holds a small package. THEY search for signs of Erichtho.

AGLAONIKE

Maybe she meant a different necropolis?

Suddenly, a flash of smoke and a hiss. ERICHTHO appears from behind a statue.

ERICHTHO

I summoned and you came. Does this mean you've reconsidered?

AGLAONIKE
No, but I'd like to know the formula for smoke.

ERICHTHO
If you won't trade your soul for my secrets, what have you brought in its stead?

AGLAONIKE hands Erichtho the package.

AGLAONIKE
Grape leaves.

ERICHTHO accepts the package, opens it, and sniffs.

Yiayia's recipe, but I made them myself.

ERICHTHO
That's something.

ERICHTHO rewraps the bag and stashes it.

All right, then. Watch this.

ERICHTHO gestures toward an unlit candle and snaps her fingers to ignite a flame.

Now you try.

AGLAONIKE skeptically snaps her fingers. The flame goes out. Then TIGER sneezes, and all the candles are lit.

Just as I thought.

AGLAONIKE
The Witches of Thessaly could do that.

ERICHTHO
The women of whom you speak have inherited the title but not the sanctity of their foremothers. They cannot illume the fires in Hekate's temple. They idolize her darkness but fail to see her light.

AGLAONIKE
Hekate? Artemis' sunless sister?

ERICHTHO
The triformis goddess has multiple faces: Hekate, Artemis, and Selene. The truly enlightened enchantress absorbs facets from all three.

AGLAONIKE
Like I do. I'm magical.

AGLAONIKE snaps her fingers. The flames go out. SHE snaps them again. The flames ignite.

You must have this rigged.

ERICHTHO
You have mystical powers.

AGLAONIKE
Is that why you summoned me? Don't you have your own magic?

ERICHTHO
Of course.

SHE holds up a hoop and creates the flickering illusion of a Tigress within it. It shimmers in the moonlight. TIGER approaches it with interest.

But an arrangement between us could be mutually beneficial.

ERICHTHO lowers the hoop. The illusion disappears. TIGER deflates.

AGLAONIKE
Another illusion.

ERICHTHO
The cat yearns to know his own kind.

AGLAONIKE

I am his own kind.

SHE puts her arms around Tiger.

ERICHTHO

One day, he'll feel the primal call, the feline urge to roam and hunt and mate. He's a creature of the jungle.

AGLAONIKE

He'd never leave me.

ERICHTHO

You seem eager to learn till you find the facts disagreeable.

AGLAONIKE

Facts!

ERICHTHO

You forget my omniscience.

AGLAONIKE

I don't forget. I disbelieve.

ERICHTHO

Blasphemous girl.

ERICHTHO begins to chant, a series of eerie hisses. Then SHE holds up the hoop. TIGER perks up and watches as the Tigress illusion reappears. ERICHTHO poses like a lion tamer, and TIGER leaps into the hoop (& maybe the hoop catches fire?). HE disappears. AGLAONIKE runs after him, but ERICHTHO slams the hoop to the ground as AGLAONIKE screams:

AGLAONIKE

Nooooooo!

AGLAONIKE attempts to grab the hoop from ERICHTHO, who silently steps inside it.

Bring him back.

ERICHTHO

He departed of his own volition. I told you what he wants, and he agreed.

AGLAONIKE

Bring him back.

ERICHTHO

And if I do?

AGLAONIKE

What do you want? Anything. Please. I'll do whatever you say.

ERICHTHO

Will you? Then swear before Hekate. Swear you'll do whatever I say.

AGLAONIKE

One thing. I'll do one thing you say.

ERICHTHO

You'll become my apprentice.

AGLAONIKE

For how long?

ERICHTHO

Forever.

AGLAONIKE

Not forever. For … one month.

ERICHTHO

You're in no position to bargain, and you know you're intrigued. But fine. We'll agree on an epoch: one year.

AGLAONIKE

One year for Tiger. Okay. Where is he?

ERICHTHO

He's safe.

AGLAONIKE

Why should I trust you?

ERICHTHO holds up the hoop, displaying a vision of TIGER dozing contentedly in some trees.

ERICHTHO

Optical evidence. Now swear to the goddess. One year for Tiger.

AGLAONIKE

(To the Hekate statue.)
I swear.

ERICHTHO

Go pack your things.

ERICHTHO vanishes. Unseen by Aglaonike, HEKATE nods. All the flames are suddenly extinguished.

End of Scene 6

Scene 7

At rise. YIAYIA scrubs the floor. SHE feels a pain in her chest. SHE dies. AGLAONIKE enters talking.

AGLAONIKE

I need help, Yiayia. I've done something bad.
Yiayia?

AGLAONIKE approaches Yiayia and touches her. SHE realizes Yiayia is dead. SHE wraps her arms around her.

Okay, Yiayia.
I'll be brave.

AGLAONIKE exits. SELENE enters and gently leads YIAYIA away.

End of Scene 7

Scene 8

At rise. The necropolis at night. Pillars, graves, a shrub. Yiayia's grave is a shrine signified by a candelabra, unlit. AGLAONIKE kneels before it. SHE holds a lit candle. A moment of silence. SHE rises to light the rest of the candles. A hiss. The candles are suddenly lit. ERICHTHO appears.

AGLAONIKE
It's my grandmother's funeral.

ERICHTHO
I can raise the dead.

AGLAONIKE
Is that why you killed her?

ERICHTHO
Killed her so I could raise her? I'm a sorceress, not a sociopath. Yiayia died of age.

AGLAONIKE
You're older than she was.

ERICHTHO
You're not going to ask me *how* I raise the dead? Isn't your little scientific mind piqued?

AGLAONIKE
What I want is to be free, and I can't get that by becoming more beholden. Bring back Tiger.

ERICHTHO

I give the orders. You're the apprentice. First things first:
We'll bring back the dead.

ERICHTHO raises her arms as if to cast a spell.

AGLAONIKE

Let her rest in peace. Please.

ERICHTHO

We'll raise someone else. Here.

SHE spins around and points to a recent grave.

Break a branch.

SHE points to a bush growing near the grave.

Do it.

AGLAONIKE breaks a branch off the shrub.

Scorch it.

ERICHTHO points to the candelabra. AGLAONIKE holds the branch in the flame of the candelabra and lights it on fire. As SHE holds the burning branch before her, ASTRONOMER 1 appears suspended above the grave. AGLAONIKE continues to hold the branch.

AGLAONIKE

(To Erichtho.)
How—?

ERICHTHO

(To Aglaonike.)
Ask *him* anything.

AGLAONIKE

Sir?

ASTRONOMER 1

What is it?

AGLAONIKE

My Yiayia … Have you seen her? I'd like to know she's okay.

ASTRONOMER 1

Hey, I remember you. You're that girl who came to ask about the moon.

AGLAONIKE

Oh! You're one of the astronomers! What happened to you?

ASTRONOMER 1

I died.

AGLAONIKE

I'm sorry.

ASTRONOMER 1

Yeah, well. Rotten pomegranate.

AGLAONIKE

You died eating fruit?

ASTRONOMER 1

I slipped on it and broke my neck.

AGLAONIKE

Oh.

ASTRONOMER 1

So what'd you raise me up for? Another interrogation?

AGLAONIKE

My Yiayia …

ASTRONOMER 1

She stuffs the best grape leaves.

AGLAONIKE

Yes that's her.

ASTRONOMER 1

This place is ten times better since she arrived. I mean … *that* place. Can I go back now? It's almost suppertime.

AGLAONIKE

Well, while you're here …

ASTRONOMER 1

Okay, look. I like your Yiayia, and you brought us wine, so I'm willing to overlook that you're a girl for just a minute. Brief lesson in astronomy. That shrine there?

HE points to the candles.

That's the sun. And you, you're the Earth, so you orbit the sun. Got it?

Moon music plays softly. AGLAONIKE walks in a wide circle around the candelabra.

ASTRONOMER 1

And you, lady—

ERICHTHO

I am the sorceress Erichtho.

ASTRONOMER 1

Okay, sorceress lady. You're the moon. That means you orbit the Earth.

ERICHTHO

I know what the moon means.

ERICHTHO circles Aglaonike.

ASTRONOMER 1

Okay, stop.

Moon music stops playing. AGLAONIKE and ERICHTHO stop moving.

Now look around. See how the sun shines on both Earth and moon? So both are illuminated. That's what the sun does. Got it? Okay, start again.

Moon music plays softly. AGLAONIKE and ERICHTHO resume their orbits. At the moment when the candelabra, AGLAONIKE, and ERICHTHO are all in a straight line (in that order), ASTRONOMER 1 speaks:

Stop.

Moon music stops playing. AGLAONIKE and ERICHTHO stop moving.

You see, girl, how the moon's in your shadow? It's like that in the sky. When they're all in a line, the sun shines on the moon, but then Earth gets in its way—and the moon seems to vanish. Briefly. We call that an eclipse. A lunar eclipse. It takes 365 days for the Earth to orbit the sun, and it takes one day for the moon to orbit the Earth. So if you want to know the frequency of the eclipse, just do the math. Got it?

AGLAONIKE

Yes, sir, but …

ASTRONOMER 1

You don't even have to do the math. You can just read my moon chart.

AGLAONIKE

I know, but … I know all this. My questions are more advanced. I want to know why sometimes the moon chart's mistaken.

ASTRONOMER 1

Now you're being ridiculous. You can't have called me here to question my legacy.

AGLAONIKE

But it's not always right.

ASTRONOMER 1

The gods don't want us to know everything.

AGLAONIKE

You mean if you can't figure something out, you just blame the gods? But this is science. It needs to make sense. I'm trying to understand.

ASTRONOMER 1

Did you hear that? Definitely the dinner bell. Your Yiayia's making moussaka.

ASTRONOMER 1 vanishes. AGLAONIKE examines the branch, which has stopped burning.

AGLAONIKE

Yiayia made the best moussaka.

ERICHTHO

So you see, science can't answer all your questions.

AGLAONIKE

Maybe science just isn't advanced enough yet.

ERICHTHO

Are you going to advance it?

AGLAONIKE

I'm going to try. What's that shrub?

ERICHTHO

When Medea flew off in her dragon chariot, her herb pouch burst open, and her magical seeds rained down to this necropolis.

AGLAONIKE

So you can burn it to raise the dead, but what happens if you eat it? Or if you make tea of it? Or if you grind it into powder? Does it flower, and if it does, have you tested the petals? Does it work differently at different times of year? I'll take a few branches, conduct a few tests.

AGLAONIKE picks a branch and tastes a leaf.

Trial and error. Cause and effect.

ERICHTHO

That vocabulary won't suit sorcery.

AGLAONIKE

The difference between science and magic is words?

ERICHTHO

Say goodbye to grandma. And then come back to me.

ERICHTHO vanishes. AGLAONIKE kneels before the shrine.

AGLAONIKE

(To the shrine.)

You told me the world is a dangerous place, but it never felt that way with you. Don't worry about me, Yiayia. I can take care of myself. But I'll miss you. And I promise to keep trying, even if I'm not sure what that means.

End of Scene 8

Scene 9

At rise. The necropolis. Darkness. Time passes as the moon twirls through phases. CHORUS 1, 2, and 3 address the audience.

CHORUS 1

While Yiayia embraced her new underworld role,
and Tiger roamed free in his mystical jungle,

CHORUS 2

Aglaonike worked hard to demystify magic,
to reduce it to formulas and pure mathematics.

CHORUS 3

She put on a brave face, all alone without Tiger.
Her obsession with logic amused her new mentor.

CHORUS 1, 2, and 3 become statues of Hekate, Selene, and Artemis. AGLAONIKE enters, twirling Erichtho's hoop. SHE examines it. SHE holds it up to the sky. SHE sprinkles powder on it. SHE blows into it. SHE steps inside it. Nothing. ERICHTHO enters.

ERICHTHO

Try mice.

AGLAONIKE

Mice?

ERICHTHO holds a mouse by its tail and hands it to Aglaonike. AGLAONIKE sets it inside the hoop and watches it disappear.

Oh! Where'd it go!? What did I do? What does it mean?

ERICHTHO

You ask the wrong questions.

AGLAONIKE

How can I make it return?

ERICHTHO

Exactly.

AGLAONIKE

If I can bring back the mouse, can I bring back Tiger?

ERICHTHO

Keep trying.

AGLAONIKE

That's what Yiayia used to say.

AGLAONIKE does some impressive gymnastic feat with the hoop. SHE pops her head into it. Nothing.

Ugh! It's just a ring!

ERICHTHO

Just a ring? You of all humans should appreciate the potency of the circlet, the efficacy of the ambit, the harness of the hoop.

AGLAONIKE

Riddles, riddles, riddles: ugh! I of all humans. Why me? What makes me special? Oh, I know: I'm a scientist! On hiatus, but still. The potency of the circlet, the circle, the … orbit. … The moon's path is an imperfect circle … An *imperfect* circle.

SHE stretches the hoop slightly and holds it up vertically. A mouse jumps out and runs away.

A mouse! I did it! I brought it back. Is imperfection the answer?

ERICHTHO

What else can you do?

AGLAONIKE stretches the hoop. Unseen by Aglaonike, ARTEMIS nods. TIGER emerges from the hoop.

Tiger!

AGLAONIKE and TIGER hug and dance silently, preoccupied with their reunion, as HEKATE, SELENE, and ARTEMIS revert to Chorus 1, 2, and 3.

CHORUS 3

The next months passed quickly; the three lived in accord.
Student heeded mentor and hung on her words.

ERICHTHO enters, regally. AGLAONIKE and TIGER sit at her feet as if to absorb to her brilliance. After a brief tableau, the CHORUS continues.

CHORUS 1

Erichtho's night ritual was brushing the tiger.
He enjoyed the sensation while shedding his striped fur.

ERICHTHO holds up a silver hairbrush and brushes Tiger.

CHORUS 2

Meanwhile the girl monitored lunar rotations
and derived astronomical abstract equations.

AGLAONIKE scribbles equations, crosses them out, studies the sky, and scribbles some more.

CHORUS 3

She saw the moon moved fastest near Earth
but slowed in the distant skies of its girth.

CHORUS 1

Then the mentor objected: Too much mathematics,
and dazzled her student with some fresh hocus pocus.

ERICHTHO causes a tiny explosion. AGLAONIKE is intrigued. ERICHTHO hands her a vial. AGLAONIKE sniffs it. AGLAONIKE mixes formulas. TIGER assists.

CHORUS 2

She mixed viscous and frothy blood-red concoctions
and chanted dark spells with a convert's devotion.

AGLAONIKE

(Holding up a beaker.)
Black tar blackberry black pit of despair,
Mix six daktylos swamp water with one tiger hair.

SHE plucks a hair from Tiger and adds it to the beaker. The contents change color. TIGER applauds.

CHORUS 3

Her potions caused minor phenomena to occur,
from unearthly projections to spontaneous weather.

A clap of thunder. Then: AGLAONIKE holds up a mouse by its tail.

AGLAONIKE

(To Tiger.)
I wonder where the mice go, where I send them.
(Pause.)
I know. Let's paint them pink. That way, if we see them again, we'll recognize them.

TIGER grabs the mouse and finds a paintbrush. HE twirls around with them. AGLAONIKE resumes her experiments.

CHORUS 1

The problem was none of it made any sense.
Nothing could be explained by science.

AGLAONIKE

(Throwing her hands up in frustration.)
I don't get it!

CHORUS 2

No matter how exactly she tested ingredients,
she could never determine what made them expedient.

CHORUS 3

Therefore, one year later, at the end of her servitude,
of her magic she maintained her skeptical attitude.

A full moon suddenly appears. (Or: A moon has been present throughout the scene, but it's gone through all its phases, starting and ending up full.) CHORUS 1, 2, and 3 step back and watch the rest of the scene unfold. AGLAONIKE begins to pack a small suitcase.

AGLAONIKE

(To Erichtho.)
I still don't understand how anything works, and I still don't understand why you wanted to teach me.

ERICHTHO

You don't need to understand. You're a sorceress now.

AGLAONIKE

Why would you want the competition?

ERICHTHO

You'll see.

AGLAONIKE

Well, anyway. Thank you.

ERICHTHO

Your father's at war. Your grandmother's gone. Most women your age are married.

AGLAONIKE

Most women your age are dead.

AGLAONIKE zips up her suitcase.

I'll send you a postcard.

ERICHTHO

That's not necessary. I'll know where you are. You'll draw attention: You have a tiger. Unless you'd like to leave him with me?

AGLAONIKE

He doesn't like you.

ERICHTHO

Nor do you. But you'll miss me just the same.

AGLAONIKE ties a red ribbon to Tiger. Tiger music plays. AGLAONIKE and TIGER tango as THEY exit. CHORUS 1, 2, and 3 exit, tangoing. ERICHTHO raises a hand to signal the music, which suddenly stops. SHE pulls out an enormous sack of fur, quite full, and holds it up, triumphant.

End of Scene 9

Scene 10

At rise. Outside the tent of the Witches of Thessaly. The rope-and-pulley system is hooked up like before. In front of the tent, a sign: "Lunar Eclipse. 10 Drachmas." WITCH 1 and WITCH 2 (puppets) sell tickets. WITCH 2 wears an eye patch. AGLAONIKE and TIGER approach. AGLAONIKE carries her suitcase.

WITCH 1

One night only!

WITCH 2

Standing-room only!

AGLAONIKE

A lunar eclipse? Tonight? That's impossible.

WITCH 1

You again.

WITCH 2

(To Witch 1.)

Her again.

WITCH 1

Last time you were here, you scared away our customers.

AGLAONIKE

You scared your customers! Wasn't that what you wanted?

WITCH 2

We wanted them to be scared. Not scared away. Scared *away* doesn't pay the rent.

WITCH 1

But that's okay. We're delighted to see you.

WITCH 2

We were hoping you'd come.

WITCH 1

We've been waiting a while.

WITCH 2

Perhaps you'd care for a cup of tea?

WITCH 1

Never let it be said we're not gracious.

WITCH 1 and WITCH 2 cackle. WITCH 3 (human) enters surreptitiously and starts fiddling with the rope-and-pulley system. AGLAONIKE doesn't notice her. (TIGER might.)

AGLAONIKE

I see you've raised your price.

WITCH 2

Inflation.

WITCH 1

Too rich for your wallet?

AGLAONIKE

I've seen your show.

WITCH 2

Lots of people come to see it again.

WITCH 1

Some every week.

AGLAONIKE

Why would they do that?

WITCH 1

We provide an essential service to the community.

AGLAONIKE

You're a menace to society. Come on, Tiger.

WITCH 1

What's your hurry? Are you going somewhere?

WITCH 2

Or are you on your way home?

AGLAONIKE

Neither.

WITCH 1

Ooh, cryptic. We like that.

WITCH 2

You know, haughty girl, most people are afraid of us.

WITCH 1

Of course, most people are afraid of you, too. Well, they're afraid of your tiger.

TIGER growls. WITCH 1 and WITCH 2 quiver and titter.

WITCH 1

Ooh, scary. We like that.

WITCH 2 glances over at WITCH 3, who nods.

WITCH 2

(To Aglaonike.)
Would you mind taking three steps to the left? Just the girl?

AGLAONIKE

What for?

AGLAONIKE takes Tiger's paw.

WITCH 1

Please step away from the cat.

AGLAONIKE

We're leaving.

WITCH 2

Have it your way.

WITCH 3 jumps back from the pulley system. We hear a loud squeak, and suddenly a cage falls down and encloses Aglaonike and Tiger. TIGER roars.

AGLAONIKE

What are you doing? Let us out of here!

AGLAONIKE grips the bars and shakes them. TIGER paces like an animal in a cage.

WITCH 1

We like our fear contained.

WITCH 2

Better for business.

The WITCHES cackle. WITCH 3 covers the sign with a new sign: "Terrible Tiger. 12 Drachmas."

AGLAONIKE

Let us out!

WITCH 1

We think not.

AGLAONIKE

Let *me* out then. Just me. You didn't mean to trap me anyway.

TIGER growls at Aglaonike.

WITCH 2

We didn't mean to, but we're glad we did.

WITCH 1

After all, what do tigers eat?

WITCH 2

Meat!

As WITCH 1 and WITCH 2 cackle with glee, WITCH 3 uses a marker to cross out the sign and write: "Tiger Eats Girl. 20 Drachmas."

End of Scene 10

Scene 11

At rise. Morning. AGLAONIKE and TIGER inside the cage. The suitcase is still there. TIGER paces.

AGLAONIKE

Thank you for not eating me.

TIGER ignores Aglaonike.

I'm sure they'll give you another shot tonight. Or you could get it over with now.

HE pauses to consider this option.

I wasn't going to just leave you. I was going to get help.

HE resumes pacing.

I love you. I'd never leave you.

HE ignores her.

You think it's my fault we're in here.
It's not my fault. Is it?
Can't you stop pacing? Can't we just sleep? I'm so tired.

SHE lies on the ground. HE approaches her and growls.

You're supposed to protect me.

HE might be dangerous. SHE gets up.

Even if you eat me, they won't free you. They'd just find someone else to feed to you. How will we get out of here? Wouldn't it be great if … Wait! I have an idea. I'll use magic. I'll make like we're mice! I'm not a sorceress for nothing.

SHE opens the suitcase and begins rummaging through it. As she finds each ingredient, she slowly says its name aloud.

One drop of narcissus nectar. One hyacinth petal. One sunflower stamen. Beak of a swan, powdered. Half a mollusk shell, shattered. One wagtail feather, ground to dust. One saffron thread. Four fingers of fermented barley water. Juice of one white mushroom … You know what I'm missing? This is so ridiculous. I'm missing a grape.

TIGER paces.

A grape, Tiger. All I need's a grape. I didn't bother to pack any because they're so easy to find.

HE growls at her.

I think I could do it. I could make us disappear. I've never done it before, but it's time to be brave. The pink mice came back when I called them. They were fine. Didn't they seem fine to you? You ate them. Did they taste strange?

HE stops pacing and stares at her.

All I need is one grape. I guess they're not likely to bring us breakfast. They'll want to keep you hungry.

SHE kneels and prays.

Oh mighty Artemis. I know it's been a while since last time I prayed, but I really need your help. And it's not just for myself but for Tiger—the kitten you gave me through the oracle. He's all grown up now, and he's my best friend, and we're trapped in a cage and we need to get out before he … starves to death. I think I could get us out myself if I only had a grape. If you could send one my way, I'll be grateful forever.

Enter WITCH 3 with a fruit platter.

Thank you, Artemis!

AGLAONIKE rises. WITCH 3 walks right past the cage without stopping.

Wait!

WITCH 3 pauses.

I'm hungry.

WITCH 3

You put on a lousy show last night. You were supposed to get eaten, and instead you droned on about equations.

AGLAONIKE

The audience seemed interested.

WITCH 3

They were interested to see if you'd die a slow and bloody death.

AGLAONIKE

Maybe they'll come back tonight to find out.

WITCH 3

If you get mauled tonight, I'll give you fruit.

WITCH 3 exits.

AGLAONIKE

(To Tiger.)
Now what?

TIGER spots something on the ground right outside the cage. HE roars.

What is it? A grape! It's a grape! It must have fallen off the witch's platter. Can you reach it?

THEY both bend down and reach through the bars, trying to get the grape. Neither is successful.

It's too far. Wait! I know.

SHE reaches into her suitcase and finds a long feather. SHE pokes it through the bars and gently rolls the grape. TIGER growls.

It must be unblemished. Slowly, slowly … I've got it. I got it! It's perfect!

SHE holds up the grape and kisses Tiger. HE lets her.

Okay. I need to get everything together. All the ingredients in one vial …

SHE takes a vial from the suitcase, and as she hurriedly names each ingredient, she pours it into the container.

One drop of narcissus nectar. One hyacinth petal. One sunflower stamen. One beetle wing. Beak of a swan, powdered. Half a mollusk shell, shattered. One wagtail feather, ground to dust. One saffron thread. Four fingers of fermented barley water. Juice of one white mushroom. And …

SHE smashes the grape between her fingers and adds it to the vial.

One grape!

SHE corks the vial.

Now shake.

SHE shakes the vial.

And finally, the incantation.

SHE dangles the vial before Tiger's mouth. HE roars.

Are you ready? Here we go!

SHE holds up the vial to Tiger's lips as HE drinks. Then SHE drinks and caps what remains. THEY wait, staring at each other in silence. After a long, awkward moment, THEY vanish.

<u>End of Scene *11*</u>

Scene 12

At rise. Darkness. Silence. A flash of lightning, and we're in the Elysian Fields. A picnic blanket is spread on the ground, and YIAYIA kneels, serving food from a basket. ASTRONOMER 1 and HARRY sit on the blanket, eagerly awaiting dinner. Suddenly, AGLAONIKE and TIGER appear. AGLAONIKE clutches her suitcase.

YIAYIA

Good, you're here. We almost started without you.

AGLAONIKE

Yiayia! I've missed you.

AGLAONIKE and YIAYIA embrace. Then AGALONIKE notices Astronomer 1 and Harry.

Mr. Astronomer?

ASTRONOMER 1

Nice to see you again.

AGLAONIKE

Are we ... ? Did I ...? Kill us?

YIAYIA

No, no. You're just passing through.

AGLAONIKE

Passing through Hades? On our way to where?

YIAYIA

Who knows? You must be hungry. Luckily you've landed in our favorite picnic spot: the Elysian Fields.

AGLAONIKE and TIGER sit as YIAYIA fills their plates. HARRY shakes Aglaonike's hand.

HARRY

Welcome to the underworld. I'm Harry.

AGLAONIKE is about to introduce herself and Tiger, but HARRY cuts her off.

I know: girl genius. Yiayia yaks about you all the time.

AGLAONIKE

You call her Yiayia, too?

HARRY

She's everyone's Yiayia now. *Salud!*

HARRY and ASTRONOMER 1 stuff forkfuls of food into their mouths. AGLAONIKE and TIGER watch them.

YIAYIA

(To Aglaonike and Tiger.)
Eat up. I made it for you.

TIGER eats. AGLAONIKE doesn't.

AGLAONIKE

Why did you summon me?

YIAYIA

You summoned yourself, but I was hoping to see you.

AGLAONIKE

I don't understand.

YIAYIA

I wanted to tell you: Be brave. And keep trying.

AGLAONIKE

Trying what? You never say. Nothing makes sense.

ASTRONOMER 1
Don't ask me. I'm eating.

YIAYIA
Keep trying. Now eat up.

AGLAONIKE
But—

YIAYIA
Eat.

Something on the ground catches TIGER's attention. AGLAONIKE follows his gaze.

AGLAONIKE
A mouse. A pink mouse!

YIAYIA
You're not afraid of mice, Aglaonike? I raised you better than that.

AGLAONIKE
I'm not afraid of anything.

ASTRONOMER 1
We see them all the time. They come and go.

AGLAONIKE
I really can do magic.

YIAYIA
Is that a good thing?

AGLAONIKE
Check this out, Yiayia.

AGLAONIKE lifts the mouse off the ground and holds it up by its tail.

To some other realm, attend thee, pink rodent.

I wish ye safe travels: This potion is potent.

SHE holds up a vial.

YIAYIA

Be careful!

AGLAONIKE

I thought you wanted me to be brave.

SHE uncaps the vial. Suddenly: darkness, lightning, thunder.

End of Scene 12

Scene 13

At rise. Lights up on a battlefield in Babylon. AGLAONIKE and TIGER sit on the ground. THREE WARRIORS (WARRIOR 1, WARRIOR 2, and HEGETOR) kneel like statues, their weapons aimed at Aglaonike and Tiger. The mouse scurries off.

WARRIOR 1

They don't look like the enemy.

WARRIOR 2

They're in disguise.

WARRIOR 1

As a girl and a tiger?

HEGETOR

Capture them both. Cage the tiger.

AGLAONIKE

No.

SHE steps in front of Tiger. Now the weapons are aimed solely at her.

WARRIOR 2

Feisty.

AGLAONIKE

We're not the enemy.

WARRIOR 1

She speaks our language.

WARRIOR 2

Where are you from, girl?

AGLAONIKE

Thessaly.

WARRIOR 1

Thessaly? How did you get here?

AGLAONIKE

I concocted a formula …

WARRIOR 2

A magical formula?

AGLAONIKE

No, not magic. Science.

WARRIOR 1

What's the difference?

AGLAONIKE

Science has a rational explanation. Even if I don't know what it is yet.

HEGETOR

That sounds like something my daughter would say.

AGLAONIKE

Daddy?

HEGETOR

Aglaonike?

AGLAONIKE

Daddy!

HEGETOR

Aglaonike!

The WARRIORS aim their weapons at Tiger.

AGLAONIKE

(To the Warriors.)
Put down those weapons! He's my friend.

HEGETOR

He's a tiger. We'll take him to the king.

AGLAONIKE

No.

HEGETOR

I am in command here.

AGLAONIKE

Here. Where's here?

WARRIOR 2

Mesopotamia.

WARRIOR 1

Macedonia.

WARRIOR 2

Corinth.

WARRIOR 1

Carthage.

WARRIOR 2

Persia.

WARRIOR 1

Rome.

AGLAONIKE

You don't even know.

HEGETOR

We are often on the move.

AGLAONIKE

And never home.

HEGETOR

I serve our nation and our gods.

AGLAONIKE

You didn't recognize your own daughter. And now you want to take away my only friend. I won't let you.

SHE runs to Tiger and takes his hand. Suddenly, wind starts to blow.

WARRIOR 1

(To Hegetor.)
A word, sir?

WARRIOR 2 continues to aim his weapon at Tiger, while WARRIOR 1 and HEGETOR talk privately.

WARRIOR 1

Brave Hegetor, this is surely a sign from the gods. Our troubles and battles may end … if only you appease them.

HEGETOR

With what?

WARRIOR 1
The ultimate sacrifice. Your sole descendent.

HEGETOR
But I'm fond of her.

WARRIOR 1
That's why it's a sacrifice.

HEGETOR
Her death would prove a loss to science.

WARRIOR 1
Science! She's a girl!

HEGETOR
Remember the House of Atreus.

WARRIOR 1
Agamemnon's sacrifice of his daughter calmed the winds and let the fleet set sail.

HEGETOR
And cursed his family for eternity.

WARRIOR 1
You have no other family. There's no one to curse.

HEGETOR
Well, that's true.

WARRIOR 1
Even if Artemis doesn't want the girl, she'll surely want the tiger. As you said, sir, you serve our nation *and* our gods.

HEGETOR
You make valid points.

WARRIOR 1

And sir? One last thing. You'd be really, really famous.

HEGETOR

(To both Warriors.)
Take them to the altar.

The WARRIORS march AGLAONIKE and TIGER to a different spot. HEGETOR observes the march and then follows, grandly.

HEGETOR

(To Aglaonike and Tiger.)
Kneel, my daughter. It's time to … pray.

AGLAONIKE and TIGER kneel to pray.

But first, Aglaonike, a special present I pillaged. I've been saving it for you.

HEGETOR rummages through his armor and finds a necklace: a 6-inch disk hanging on a string. (It's an astrolabe.) HE puts it around Aglaonike's neck. SHE inspects it.

With this pendant, you can determine the date, the time, the season. See the sigma etched on top—for the second face of the moon goddess, Selene.

AGLAONIKE

How does it work?

HEGETOR

Note the gears. Note the notches on the gears. You must study and decipher them.

AGLAONIKE

I will, father.

HEGETOR

And now. Forgive me, my child, and pray. To Selene the serene, soft sister, moon queen.

AGLAONIKE and TIGER bow their heads and pray. The WARRIORS silently raise their weapons and aim at the back of their heads.

You know what?

Suddenly, HEGETOR reaches out one arm and knocks the weapons to the ground. AGLAONIKE and TIGER topple over and then sit watching as HEGETOR proclaims:

Let the winds blow.

Winds blow.

Let the rains fall.

Rains fall.

Let lightning split the skies.

Thunder, lightning: just for a moment.

I am brave Hegetor. I am not afraid of weather.

No more wind or rain.

My legacy will be pure. I shan't be tainted by hubris, remembered as vain. Your memory is selective, young warrior. Yes, when the winds were too much, Agamemnon fed them his daughter. His fleet could not cross the tempest, so he sent for the girl and promised her a hero husband. When she arrived, he appeased the winds with her blood. But that's not the whole story. Why did those winds need appeasing? Here's the part you've neglected: Artemis had made them squall as revenge against these same sailors, who'd killed her hare for sport. She loved that rabbit—alive, not dead. Let us not repeat their mistakes. Agamemnon was coerced by savage peers. His daughter was a mere girl, yet he should not have let her blood. My daughter may change the path of humankind. Artemis has eyed this child since her mother yielded to the blood of her birth. The tiny babe survived—too eager to examine her world than to let death defeat her. Her first word was not *dada* but *what*—followed by *who*, *how*, and *why*. Her favorite toy was not a doll but a sundial. She never pretended to marry a prince. She never dreamed of babes. If I promised her a hero husband, she'd say she had other plans.

HEGETOR holds out a hand to help Aglaonike rise. THEY embrace. HEGETOR stands back and takes a long, proud look at his daughter. WARRIORS 1 and 2 reclaim their weapons.

WARRIOR 1

Unnatural.

WARRIOR 2

Unfilial.

WARRIOR 1

Unholy.

WARRIORS 1 and 2 point their weapons at Hegetor. TIGER lunges to attack them, and they spin to attack to him as AGLAONIKE screams:

AGLAONIKE

Noooooooooooooooooo!

Suddenly: darkness, lightning, thunder.

End of Scene 13

Scene 14

At rise. Lights up on a creepy forest. AGLAONIKE and TIGER brush themselves off. Behind a tree, unseen: TIGRESS.

AGLAONIKE

Now what? Hegetor can take care of himself. He's not called "brave" for nothing. But what about us?

TIGER prowls, examining the shadows and trees.

"Unnatural"? "Unfilial"? "Unholy"? Me? I'm exactly what Hegetor taught me to be.

His bedtime story was Helen of Troy. Beauty leads to tragedy. No one needs to rescue me …

But what about that moon queen, Selene? He called her "serene" like that's a good thing. He said "soft" like it's a virtue, but he taught me it was weak. So he values femininity in females as long as they're not his offspring?

TIGER finds a scent that intrigues him and follows it in circles.

Tiger?

TIGER stops when he finds himself sniffing the paw of TIGRESS, who has emerged from behind the tree.

A tigress? A real, live tigress. Where on Earth are we?

AGLAONIKE jumps to her feet. TIGRESS assesses Aglaonike with disdain.

Feral, sexy. Who can blame him?

Tiger music plays. TIGER and TIGRESS dance the tango. At the end of the dance, the music stops, and TIGRESS saunters off. TIGER begins to follow.

Hey, wait. Tiger!

TIGER considers his options. HE follows Tigress and disappears into the forest.

Tiger!?

AGLAONIKE begins to follow Tiger. Suddenly: The sound of hissing snakes comes from where Tiger exited. AGLAONIKE chants as she follows:

I am not afraid. Not afraid. Not afraid. I'll be brave. Brave. Brave. Brave.

SHE is gone for a moment. Then SHE returns. SHE paces in circles as SHE muses:

Tiger gone. Can't be gone. A girl needs her tiger. A tiger needs his girl.

(Inspecting herself.)
Hands, elbows, fingers, feet, but without him I'm incomplete. I look whole but feel halved. One plus one equals two, but two minus one equals none. There's a hole in my soul—but that's illogical. The soul's intangible; it can't be torn. It's not math; it's a metaphor. Or my computation is mistaken: It's not subtraction but division. I'm not diminished but divided. I'm an illegal fraction. Aglaonike over Tiger—like a zero divisor: an impossible equation.

Sure she's a better dancer. Who wouldn't be with a swishy tail? I'd bet she's a better tree climber, too. But I can solve equations. And I can chart the moon.

(Gazing at the sky.)
Sisters of the Pleiades: Which one don't we see? There's a hole in the sky where that star should be. Maybe it's Tiger, playing hide-and-seek. Testing my bravery. Sometimes what we don't see is what we see best. That doesn't make any sense but may be true nonetheless—even if it's utterly unscientific. The moon's path is an imperfect circle, and so's mine.

AGLAONIKE sinks to the ground, where she sits with her head in her arms in silence. TIGER enters slowly. HE sits down next to Aglaonike and nudges her face with his own. SHE looks at him in wonder as he holds up his hand: It's been sliced with a claw and is trickling blood. SHE takes his wrist in her hand.

She hurt you.

Suddenly: darkness, lightning, thunder.

Again?

The lights come up on the treetop of their youth. A full moon shines. Moon music plays. AGLAONIKE and TIGER suddenly realize where they are.

Home. At last.

SHE takes his bleeding hand in her mouth. Lights out.

End of Scene 14

Scene 15

Darkness. Time passes as the moon twirls through phases. Then, at rise: the treetop, now Aglaonike's laboratory and planetarium. The tree trunk is covered with chalk markings of the moon's phases.

AGLAONIKE

What is it about barley water that makes birds fly bottoms -up? Are its inherent properties distillable? Transferable? Permutable? Hypothesis: It's not magic. Materials: Barley water. Method: We'll drink it.

TIGER growls.

I'll drink it. You'll be the control group. Procedure ...

SHE drinks the vial of barley water.

Tastes like … barley.

SHE waits a moment.

Hmmm. Nothing.

Then SHE looks at Tiger.

Tiger? There are two of you! How can that be? The barley water really is magical. Two Tigers! Wait, now there's three. Identical triplets. You look exactly alike!

Tiger Music plays. THEY begin to tango. SHE faints into Tiger's arms. TIGER gently lays her on the ground. The moon appears. Time passes. HE fans her, and SHE awakens.

So … is the barley water magical … or is it hallucinogenic? Uh oh. That could explain a lot. … Barley water was the main ingredient in our transport potion. But if we were hallucinating … where did I get this necklace?

SHE considers her pendant.

Too bad Hegetor's become a barbarian; he gives the best gifts. Look at this pendant. Its data align with the moon chart: The gears reflect the lunar graphics. I suspect it's descriptive and not prophetic. So far it's been right, but tonight *I'll* be right. That's my hypothesis, which is founded on my other hypothesis: As the moon approaches apogee, its velocity diminishes. The moon reduces its speed as it completes its orbit. It's not an optical illusion.

SHE holds up her fingers, indicating a tiny pinch.

If I'm right, the charts are wrong. Tonight, we'll see a waning crescent at 45 degrees.

SHE writes on the tree trunk.

If x equals the moon and v equals its velocity, then delta v equals …

TIGER growls. SHE stops and considers him.

Sometimes I forget we're different species. Are you part human, or am I part cat?

TIGER is poised to kiss Aglaonike, but suddenly SHE looks past him, where a crescent moon appears.

There it is—like a fiery scythe!

SHE moves so quickly that she nearly topples Tiger.

You know what this means? I can predict the moon's phases. Not just guess or estimate, but really and truly know. I'm a real scientist, and it didn't take magic. You seem vexed. You want to know: What next? That's an excellent question.

TIGER growls.

That's not your question? You don't care about the moon. You care about …

TIGER waits.

Revenge on those witches! Well, so do I. But what you haven't pieced together, dear Tiger, is that this is the means to our revenge. Of course it would be easier to eat them, but let's have fun and beat them at their own game.

SHE pulls out a piece of cardboard and writes on it, "Lunar eclipse. 5 Drachmas." TIGER's interest is piqued.

I just need an eclipse.

<u>End of Scene 15</u>

Scene 16

At rise. Dusk. The treetop and the ground below it. CHORUS 2 (Selene) is suspended in the sky: SHE is the moon. CHORUS 1 (Hekate) and CHORUS 3 (Artemis) stand below. AGLAONIKE silently scrawls her equations on the tree trunk. TIGER lies on the treetop and gazes at the stars.

CHORUS 3

From the start of our scientist's adventure-filled life,
the triformis goddess gazed on without strife.

CHORUS 1

Hekate sneered upwards from Hades' dark ditches
and reveled in the girl's hatred of make-believe witches.

CHORUS 2

Selene smiled down from her Milky Way mansion,
flattered by the stargazer's celestial passion.

CHORUS 3

Artemis, from dales and forests, prized the astronomer
for her loyalty, logic, and love of her tiger.

AGLAONIKE

(Yelling up toward the treetop.)
Tiger? I've been working on my calculations. Hypothesis: The moon's path is an imperfect circle; therefore, the lunar month is an imperfect measure. Corollary: If the lunar month is an imperfect measure, that explains why the moon charts are an imperfect recorder, and Hegetor's astrolabe is an imperfect predictor.

CHORUS 2

Imperfect!

CHORUS 1

As time passed, however, a schism occurred:
Hekate stayed amused, and Artemis honored,

CHORUS 3

but gentle Selene became ungently disturbed,
stung by the girl's mission to master her orb.

CHORUS 1

Aglaonike's investigations did this goddess affront.
She desired adulation, not a moon-knowledge hunt.

CHORUS 2 slides down to Aglaonike's level and becomes the statue of Selene. AGLAONIKE doesn't notice her.

CHORUS 3

Till now she's been fortunate to escape many troubles,
but her luck may run out if Selena's blood boils.

SELENE points to the tree. A clap of thunder is heard, and the tree shakes. TIGER falls to the ground and lands safely on all fours.

AGLAONIKE

What was that? Tiger? Are you okay? Thunder and lightning on a sunny day?

TIGER and AGLAONIKE stare up at the sky.
CHORUS 1 and 3 step back to watch the scene unfold.

An anomaly? Oh well. While you're here, let me show you what I've discovered.

SHE holds up her necklace to demonstrate.

Hegetor's astrolabe? Too simple. See? Two gears: twenty nine teeth on one and thirty on the other, one tooth per day. You choose which one to spin depending on the length of the month, but to determine the length of the month, you guess! Hence, the mistakes. However, if the gears could account for the imperfect nature of the lunar path, they could perfectly predict the moon's phases. How, you ask? Combine them: Create one gear with 59 teeth.

SHE holds up a large gear.

Here's what I've been doing while you've been asleep.

TIGER yawns.

Check out the tiny teeth: I modeled them on your baby fangs. When I put the pieces together, I'll be able to compute calculations by years, not days, to reduce fluctuation in patterns. I'll create multiple wheels that spin simultaneously to mitigate inconsistencies. And finally, the ingenious part: The gears will spin on different axles. They won't have the same center if they're imperfect circles. My math reflects the path of the moon!

SELENE raises an arm in anger. A clap of thunder. TIGER hides.

Now if only I could predict the weather.

AGLAONIKE notices the statue.

Where did that come from?

AGLAONIKE inspects the statue.

SELENE

I am the moon queen.

AGLAONIKE kneels.

AGLAONIKE

Oh, wow. Selene. The serene?

SELENE

Sometimes I'm serene. Not today. No woman has just one mood. No woman likes to be pegged as one thing. I see you have a present for me.

SELENE takes the new gear and breaks it in half.

AGLAONIKE

That wasn't really meant for … I mean, it's … not quite finished.

SELENE

I was flattered by your attentions, but you've gone too far. There's a line between curiosity and conceit. No woman wants to be mastered. The lunar sphere glows with divine light—neither riddle nor challenge but a miracle in night. A woman likes to maintain mystery. A woman delights in privacy. A woman likes having her secrets.

AGLAONIKE

I'm a woman.

SELENE

Then you know. We all have dark sides. Some nights you see me; some nights you don't.

AGLAONIKE

That's because the sun and shadows—

SELENE

That's because of my whims.

AGLAONIKE

Soft sister, moon queen …

SELENE

Soft nothing. The moon may look like creamy velvet effervescence, but in truth it's made of rock.

AGLAONIKE

Rock!? What kind of rock? Computing its density could help me determine its orbit.

SELENE

Consider this a warning.

AGLAONIKE

A warning? Did I do something wrong?

SELENE ascends to the sky.

Did she say “warning”? Maybe she said “morning.” It is almost morning. Oh well. I guess I’d better make a new gear.

End of Scene 16

Scene 17

At rise. AGLAONIKE attempts to attract the attention of passersby. TIGER watches. Moon music plays softly.

AGLAONIKE

(To the audience.)
Citizens of Thessaly: I am Aglaonike the astronomer, daughter of Hegetor. I propose we use science to tame the world. We live in fear, for we resist knowledge. Science can make us brave.

PASSERSBY 1, 2 and 3 walk by, yawning.

We fear the moon, for we cannot fathom its whims, but, ladies and gentlemen, we *can* fathom it. If we strive, we will understand, and as a result we will better ourselves. We will better our lives.

TIGER yawns.

If we study astronomy, we will also learn farming and agronomy.

(To Tiger.)
No one’s paying attention.

(To the audience.)
I can use science to predict an eclipse!

PASSERSBY 1, 2 and 3 walk by, pointing and laughing at Aglaonike.

PASSERBY 1

Listen to her. Science.

PASSERBY 2

She should be home baking baklava.

PASSERBY 3

That's how to use your equations, lady. Nuts, honey, rosewater. Work out those proportions!

AGLAONIKE

(Holding up a very large astrolabe.)

I've created an astrolabe with 59 teeth—

PASSERBY 1

(To Tiger.)

Here kitty kitty kitty kitty.

TIGER growls. PASSERSBY 1, 2 and 3 exit laughing.

AGLAONIKE

(Yelling after them.)

A full lunar eclipse next month! It's not on the charts, but it's coming.

PASSERSBY 1, 2, and 3 laugh harder, off-stage.

AGLAONIKE

(To Tiger.)

I know. I'm sorry. I just had to try science one last time.

TIGER growls.

Okay, I'll do it your way.

Moon music stops—maybe the sound of a scratchy needle. AGLAONIKE addresses the audience.

Ladies and gentlemen, I am the enchantress Aglaonike. And I have magic in me.

Witchy music plays. PASSERSBY 1, 2 and 3 enter.

PASSERBY 1
Magic?

PASSERBY 2
Did someone say "magic"?

PASSERBY 3
I love magic!

AGLAONIKE
On the ninth night of Mounichion, month of Artemis, I'll make the moon vanish.

PASSERBY 1
Ooh, I've seen that show. It never gets old.

PASSERBY 2
The one with the witches? Where they draw down the moon?

PASSERBY 3
That one lost an eye doing it. Have you seen her? She is one ugly witch, man.

PASSERBY 1
I wish I'd been there to see that.

PASSERBY 2
Let's see if we can get tickets this weekend.

AGLAONIKE
No, not that show. My show's more real.

PASSERBY 3
Real? Who wants real?

AGLAONIKE

More intense.

PASSERBY 1

I like intense, man.

AGLAONIKE

More frightening.

PASSERBY 2

Frightening! Cool!

TIGER roars.

PASSERBY 3

Frightening. Cool.

AGLAONIKE

Tiger's part of the show.

PASSERBY 1

Does he make magic?

AGLAONIKE

Tiger *is* magic.

PASSERBY 2

Oh yeah?

AGLAONIKE

Yeah. Come and see us on the ninth: Aglaonike the enchantress and her magical Tiger. Tiger will make the moon disappear.

PASSERBY 3

A cat can do that? How?

AGLAONIKE

He'll … eat it.

PASSERBY 1

He'll eat it! Ooh, this is gonna be good.

PASSERSBY 1, 2, and 3 start to leave.

AGLAONIKE

Don't forget …

PASSERBY 2

The ninth. We'll be there.

PASSERBY 3

(To Passersby 1 and 2.)
That tiger's gonna eat the moon, man.

PASSERSBY 1, 2, and 3 exit.

AGLAONIKE

Tiger's gonna eat the moon. Man.

End of Scene 17

Scene 18

At rise. Hades. AGLAONIKE lies asleep on the ground. SHE awakens suddenly. YIAYIA enters, sweeping.

YIAYIA

Are you back, Aglaonike? A girl shouldn't spend so much time in Hades.

AGLAONIKE

I'm not a girl anymore, Yiayia. And I'm not in Hades. I'm in a dream. Where's Tiger?

YIAYIA

He has his own dreams.

AGLAONIKE

Without me?

YIAYIA

You can't draw down the moon, Aglaonike. You know that.

AGLAONIKE

But I can predict an eclipse—a full lunar dark eclipse. I keep trying to tell people, but no one listens.

YIAYIA

They're listening now—and not just people.

AGLAONIKE

You mean the gods?

YIAYIA

Be careful, granddaughter. It's hubris.

AGLAONIKE

It's science.

YIAYIA

Same thing.

AGLAONIKE

The witches say you can lose an eye…?

YIAYIA

You may lose something more important.

YIAYIA vanishes.

AGLAONIKE

Yiayia? Where'd you go? Yiayia? Come back.

Silence. Then: the sound of hissing snakes. ERICHTHO appears. SHE wears a striped sweater and scarf spun of tiger fur.

The sorceress Erichtho!

ERICHTHO

The enchantress Aglaonike. You're causing quite a stir. You owe me much gratitude for the gifts I've conferred. Fortunately, the opportunity to mold a voracious mind offers satisfaction beyond thanks.

AGLAONIKE

What are you wearing?

ERICHTHO

Your Tiger.

AGLAONIKE

What have you done with him?

ERICHTHO

You always assume the worst.

ERICHTHO hisses as darkness descends.

End of Scene 18

Scene 19

At rise. A full moon rising above an incline. At ground level, AGLAONIKE and TIGER stand facing each other.

AGLAONIKE

It's the ninth night of Mounichion, month of Artemis, moment of truth.

THEY look at each other and decide:

We may be afraid, but we'll be brave. Showtime!

Tiger music plays. TIGER steps towards Aglaonike. THEY tango. THEY bow. When the applause dies down, TIGER kneels, and like a magician about to perform a trick, AGLAONIKE ties a long red ribbon to Tiger. SHE grabs the end of the ribbon and holds it up in the air. SHE and TIGER stand facing the audience.

(To the audience.)
I am Aglaonike the enchantress, and this is Tiger, my familiar. Tonight, together, we'll make the moon disappear.

WITCH 1 and WITCH 2 (puppets) enter. AGLAONIKE lowers her arm holding Tiger's ribbon.

WITCH 1

So this is where our audience went.

WITCH 2

Stealing our show. Thief!

WITCH 1

Doesn't know how it's done. *En plein air*? *Sans* tent? That's a mistake.

WITCH 2

Someone might lose an eye!

WITCH 1 and WITCH 2 cackle.

AGLAONIKE

(To the Witches.)
If you're going to be disruptive, I'll have to ask you to leave.

WITCH 1 and WITCH 2 cackle louder. TIGER roars at them. THEY stop.

WITCH 1

Sorry.

AGLAONIKE

(To the audience—again holding up Tiger's ribbon.)
We have between us magical powers
conferred upon us in our youthful hours.

By night Tiger eyes the constellations
seeking bobcat, cougar, or mountain lion.

The celestial forest is his favorite milieu.
He feels more at home there than down here with you.

Moon music plays. AGLAONIKE tugs the ribbon and releases it as TIGER suddenly jumps in the air and spirals. When HE lands, the ribbon is wrapped around him. AGLAONIKE unravels the ribbon and then leans in closely to TIGER's face as if to kiss him. SHE unties his ribbon, folds it up, and pockets it. AGLAONIKE looks at the moon.

Now, my fellow Thessalians, without much ado,
Tiger and I will vanish the moon.

TIGER pounces on all fours to the top of the incline. HE stands there and stares at the moon, poised as if ready to leap. Moon music stops. Silence. The moon turns red, as if filling with blood. The moon turns black. Darkness.

AUDIENCE

(CHORUS 1, 2, and 3: voices piped in.)
It's the end of the world!
Drought!
Starvation!
Disease!
The deaths of kings!
Run for your lives!

The sound of running footsteps exiting.

(One last voice.)
Those witches don't know diddly!

WITCH 1

Damn her.

WITCH 2

Now no one's gonna wanna see our ē-clipse.

WITCH 1

We're out of business.

WITCH 2

We're outta here!

The sound of puppet footsteps exiting. Lights up. AGLAONIKE stands looking up at the (no-longer-red) moon. ERICHTHO stands off to the side, wearing her tiger-striped sweater and a tiger-striped scarf.

AGLAONIKE

Tiger? Tiger!

ERICHTHO

He's off with the ocelots.

AGLAONIKE looks at Erichtho.

He never belonged here. You knew that.

AGLAONIKE

What did you do?

ERICHTHO

I watched. I enjoyed the show. Thank you: I've wanted to take down those witches for years.

AGLAONIKE

Then why didn't you?

ERICHTHO

Didn't I?

AGLAONIKE

This was your plan all along.

ERICHTHO

Hekate is pleased with you.

AGLAONIKE
Well, someone's not.

ERICHTHO
You mean Selene. The moon queen. Who knew she had a jealous streak? Then again, she did warn you.

AGLAONIKE
She took my Tiger?

ERICHTHO
Oh, Aglaonike. What happened to science? Maybe your Tiger walked away.

ERICHTHO spins to show off her sweater.

I spun his fur into yarn. It keeps me quite warm.

AGLAONIKE
What else does it do?

ERICHTHO
Not everything's magic. Here, I made this for you.

SHE wraps her scarf around Aglaonike's neck.

Something to remember us by.

ERICHTHO laughs as she exits (walking) to the sound of hissing snakes,

AGLAONIKE
(To herself.)
Tiger.

End of Scene 19

Scene 20

Darkness. Time passes as the moon twirls through phases. Lots of phases. Then, at rise: Dusk. A crescent moon shines above Aglaonike's tree. AGLAONIKE sits under the tree. SHE wears her tiger-striped scarf. The sound of an owl screeching. HESPER enters. The owl, STRIX (a puppet) sits on her shoulder.

HESPER

Excuse me? Are you astronomer who predicted the dark lunar eclipse that defeated the witches?

AGLAONIKE

No, I'm the enchantress who traded her tiger for a magic trick. Long before you were born.

HESPER

It's been only seventy lunar months since then. I'm older than that.

AGLAONIKE

Seems longer.

HESPER

I was hoping you'd explain the science. I was hoping you'd teach me.

AGLAONIKE

I'm afraid, little girl, that you're in the wrong place.

HESPER

The oracle told me to seek you.

AGLAONIKE

What oracle?

HESPER

The one who gave me the owl. Said it was from Selene.

AGLAONIKE
Selene's oracle gave you an owl and sent you to see me?

HESPER
(She means the owl.)
His name is Strix.

STRIX makes an owl noise.

AGLAONIKE
What does he do?

HESPER
He can see in the dark and hunt mice.

AGLAONIKE
He can't do magic?

HESPER
Of course not.

AGLAONIKE
Is he your best friend?

HESPER
He's a bird.

STRIX jumps onto Aglaonike's shoulder.

He likes you.

AGLAONIKE
I thought owls were from Athena.

HESPER
Not this one.

AGLAONIKE
What is it you want to learn?

HESPER

Why the moon charts are wrong. And how you knew they would be.

AGLAONIKE

Witchcraft.

HESPER

Science. The Witches of Thessaly were dragged through the streets. That didn't happen to you.

AGLAONIKE

I had better role models. What's your name, little girl?

HESPER

My name is Hesper, and I want you to teach me the stars.

AGLAONIKE

Don't you have a mother?

HESPER

I'm not looking for a family. I'm looking for an education.

AGLAONIKE

Then why visit the oracle?

HESPER

What do you mean?

AGLAONIKE

You're skeptical about magic, yet you sought out a seer.

HESPER

I seek knowledge everywhere I go. And I listen to whatever I'm told. Though I don't always believe it.

AGLAONIKE

What did he tell you, this seer?

HESPER

It was a woman.

AGLAONIKE
What did she tell you?

HESPER
To find you. To learn from you. And to give you this message: Be brave.

AGLAONIKE
Be brave.

HESPER
She also said to keep trying.

AGLAONIKE
Trying what?

HESPER
She didn't say, but isn't it obvious? Keep trying everything. If you want to know science, keep conducting experiments. If you want to know math, keep deriving equations. If you want someone to teach you, keep asking till she agrees. Keep trying till you get it right—and then, try something new.

AGLAONIKE
Did she say anything else?

HESPER
She said that the deity misses your attentions.

AGLAONIKE
Selene?

HESPER
Yes.

AGLAONIKE
That is one fickle goddess.

HESPER

She said that's a woman's prerogative.

AGLAONIKE

You should go home now, Hesper.

HESPER

First can I climb your tree?

AGLAONIKE

No.

HESPER

It looks like a good place to stargaze.

THEY look up.

I wonder about the Pleiades. Orion stalked seven sisters, and they escaped to the sky. I see only six. Did he catch one?

AGLAONIKE

I've wondered that myself.

STRIX flies up into the tree. HE hoots and hops around the leaves.

HESPER

He likes it here. Please can we stay? Just a little while?

An object falls from the tree: a rolled-up paper. HESPER catches it and unrolls it.

Papyrus. A formula?

AGLAONIKE

Yiayia's recipe for grape leaves.

HESPER

I love grape leaves.

AGLAONIKE
Me too.

A large astrolabe falls from the tree. HESPER catches it.

HESPER
An astrolabe?

AGLAONIKE
You've seen one before?

HESPER
This one's different. Bigger. Extra gears. Twice the teeth?

AGLAONIKE
Not quite. Count them.

HESPER counts the teeth.

HESPER
Fifty-nine? An odd number. What does it mean?

AGLAONIKE
Think about it. Develop a hypothesis. Start with the number of days …

HESPER studies the astrolabe.

HESPER
Two lunar months: 30 plus 29 days. So it's not an approximation …

AGLAONIKE
In science, you need to be exact.

HESPER
I want to learn everything.

AGLAONIKE

First lesson: We can't know everything.

HESPER

"I propose that we use science to tame the world," your words.

AGLAONIKE

Keep trying.

A red ribbon floats from the tree to Aglaonike. It's tied into a loop with a bow, like a necktie without a neck. HESPER looks up as AGLAONIKE catches it.

HESPER

A ribbon.

AGLAONIKE

Tiger. He's a star in the sky.

AGLAONIKE holds the ribbon high and looks upwards, through the loop.

The moon's path is an imperfect circle, and so's mine.

STRIX flies down through the loop of the ribbon, so that the bow's around his neck. As HE flies off wearing it, HE screeches.

<u>End of Play</u>

Works Consulted

Azarpay, G. and A.D. Kilmer. "The Eclipse Dragon on an Arabic Frontispiece-Miniature." *Journal of the American Oriental Society* 98.4 (1978): 363-374.

Bicknell, Peter. "The Witch Aglaonice and Dark Lunar Eclipses in the Second and First Centuries BC." *Journal of the British Astronomical Association* 93.4 (1983): 160-63.

---. "The Dark Side of the Moon." *MAISTOR: Classical, Byzantine and Renaissance Studies for Robert Browning*. Canberra: The Australian Association for Byzantine Studies, 1984. 67-75.

Bodson, Liliane. "Ancient Greek Views on the Exotic Animal." *Arctos: Acta Philologia Fennica* 32 (1998): 61-85.

Cantarella, Eva. "Dangling Virgins: Myth, Ritual and the Place of Women in Ancient Greece." *Poetics Today* 6.1-2 (1985): 91-101.

"Closs, Michael P. "Cognitive Aspects of Ancient Maya Eclipse Theory." *World Archaeoastronomy: Selected Papers from the 2nd Oxford International Conference on Archaeoastronomy*. Ed. Anthony F. Aveni. Cambridge: Cambridge UP, 1988. E-book.

Cocteau, Jean. *Orpheus*. Trans. John Savacool. *The Infernal Machine and Other Plays by Jean Cocteau*. New York: New Directions, 1963. 97-150.

Dicks, D.R. *Early Greek Astronomy to Aristotle*. Ithaca: Cornell UP, 1970.

Freeth, Tony. "Decoding an Ancient Computer." *Scientific American* Dec. 2009: 76-83.

Freeth, Tony, et al. "Decoding the Ancient Greek Astronomical Calculator known as the Antikythera Mechanism." *Nature* 30 Nov. 2006: 587-91.

Ginzburg, Carlos. "Darkness and Din." *Interdisciplinary Science Reviews* 35.3-4 (2010): 266-76.

Godwin, E.W. "Erichtho." *The Haunters & The Haunted Ghost Stories and Tales of the Supernatural*. Ed. Ernest Rhys. London: O'Connor, 1921. Amazon Digital: 2011.

Greenblatt, Stephen. *The Swerve: How the World Became Modern*. New York: Norton, 2011.

Hamilton, Edith. *Mythology*. 1942. New York: Little, 1998.

Hill, D. E. "The Thessalian Trick." *Rheinisches Museum für Philologie* 116 (1973): 221-38.

Hoyt, Olga. *Witches*. New York: Abelard-Schuman, 1969.

Khachadourian, Diana. "Scholars and Sorceresses: Ancient Women Astronomers." *Women in Astronomy and Space Science: Proceedings from the Conference*. Ed. Anna L. Kinney et al. NASA, 2009: 283-89. Web 3 Oct. 2012.

León, Vicki. *How to Mellify a Corpse and Other Human Stories of Ancient Science and Superstition*. New York: Walker, 2010.

Milbrath, S. "Eclipse Imagery in Mexica Sculpture of Central Mexico." *Vistas in Astronomy* 39 (1995): 479-502.

Montelle, Clemency. *Chasing Shadows: Mathematics, Astronomy, and the Early History of Eclipse Reckoning*. Baltimore: Johns Hopkins UP, 2011.

Ogilvie, Marilyn Bailey. *Women in Science: Antiquity through the Nineteenth Century*. Cambridge, MA: MIT P, 1990.

Phillips, Oliver. *Magic and Ritual in the Ancient World*. Ed. Paul Allan Mirecki and Marvin W. Meyer. Boston: Brill, 2002. E-book.

Plutarch. "Why the Oracles Cease to Give Answers." *Moralia* vol. 4. *The Complete Works of Plutarch*. Trans. John Dryden. Amazon Digital/Charles River, 2011.

Rabinowitz, Jacob. *The Rotting Goddess: The Origin of the Witch in Classical Antiquity*. Brooklyn: Autonomedia, 1998.

Rosser, Sue V., Ed. *Women, Science, and Myth: Gender Beliefs from Antiquity to the Present*. Denver: ABC-CLIO, 2008.

Sherwin-White, Susan and Amélie Kuhrt. *From Samarkhand to Sardis: A New Approach to the Seleucid Empire*. Berkeley: U California P, 1993.

Skelhorn, Angie. "The Ancient Witches of Thessaly." Web. 23 Sept. 2012.

Stothers, Richard B. "Dark Lunar Eclipses in Classical Antiquity." *Journal of the British Astronomical Association* 96.2 (1986): 95-97.

Trejo, J. Galindo. "The Astronomy in the Mexican Prehispanic Past." *Galaxies: The Third Dimension*. ASP Conference Series 282 (2002): 3-15.

Vallianatos, Evaggelos. "Deciphering and Appeasing the Heavens: The History and Fate of an Ancient Greek Computer." *Leonardo* 49.3 (2012): 251-57.

NOTES

Made in the USA
Columbia, SC
29 October 2024

44967416R00057